The Perils of Imprudent Writing:

How to Watch What You Write and Stay Out of Court

Edward P. Ahrens, Jr.
Attorney at Law

Manufactured in the United States of America.

Library of Congress Catalog Number
97-90626
ISBN 0-9658381-3-7

What They're Saying about Ed Ahrens' article, "The Perils of Imprudent Writing"

LEVI STRAUSS & CO.—"....[T]hank you for permission to reprint your article for internal training purposes.[K]eep me advised on the status of your book on the same subject. I now...ask your permission to use the article on an as-needed internal basis in...advising my internal customers on business practices. From time to time I receive inquiries about 'Should we be writing this down?' (or, worse, see documents I wish hadn't been written), and your article would be a useful tool in responding, as well as providing a checklist for thinking processes."

IMMUNEX CORPORATION—"[T]his is the most succinct and to the point article I have seen on the subject matter and I feel it is one that will be well received by our managers and other employees who are going through the 'education' process."

TEXAS INSTRUMENTS—"I have just read your pithy and persuasive article....TI has developed a cluster of training courses titled 'Writing for Posterity.'...I would like your permission for TI to...distribute your article as an adjunct to the course."

REICHHOLD CHEMICALS, INC.—"I received many comments about how useful the article was and particularly about its practical, no nonsense style. It was a big hit!...I am confident that our employees will also find your article highly instructive..."

NMB (USA) INC.—"I really enjoyed your article...[It is] excellent and I am writing to seek your permission to distribute copies of it internally at a Controller's Conference for finance executives of the NMB (USA) Inc. group companies.... I look forward to...your book on this subject."

HUGHES SPACE & COMMUNICATIONS GROUP—"[T]hank you...for providing industry with your timely and useful guidance."

ARCO CHEMICAL COMPANY—"[Y]ou will be pleased to know that your writings are still providing guidance in remote locations."

FIRST AMERICAN TITLE INSURANCE COMPANY—"I just wanted you to know how much I enjoyed your article in the ACCA Docket..."

ITT— "As Southeast Regional Counsel..., I am responsible for training programs for new frontline operations supervisors, and part of that training will correspond... closely to the coverage of your article...[which will be used as] routine training material."

MOBIL OIL CORPORATION—"I would like to distribute approximately 30 copies [of your article] at an in-house Virginia CLE Study course for attorneys..."

DEGUSSA CORPORATION—"We will be using [your article] for an In-House Preventative Training Program and are confident our business people will appreciate your direct and practical advice."

STAR ENTERPRISE—"This letter requests your approval to include your excellent article...as part of the course materials I will provide during...Government Institute's July 1993 Health and Safety Auditing seminar in Hilton Head, South Carolina."

TALLEY INDUSTRIES—"Edward Ahrens' article...'The Perils of Imprudent Writing' struck me as an article that I would like to distribute to our managers."

FUJITSU NETWORK TRANSMISSION SYSTEMS, INC.—"Your article...is one I cut out and put in my 'training' files. I am about to embark on some extensive training for my company's management. In preparing for the program, I came across your article which, by the way, is great!"

The Moving Finger writes; and, having writ,
Moves on: nor all your Piety nor Wit
Shall lure it back to cancel half a Line,
Nor all your Tears wash out a Word of it.

—*Rubaiyat*, by Omar Khayyam

In memory of my father, Edward P.
Ahrens, Sr., whose example and encouragement
caused me to become an attorney but whose
passing in 1990 denied him the pleasure of
knowing I can write, too.
This one's for you, Pop.

Acknowledgements

No worthwhile writing effort, which I hope this turns out to be, is ever accomplished without the inspiration and assistance of others.

I owe debts of gratitude to Mary May Burruss and Paddy Richardson, both of whose literary genius put mine to shame and who provided me essential guidance regarding grammatical structure and stylistic techniques. When they undertook these tasks, they reminded me their talents lie in fiction. I reminded them I am an attorney.

I am equally grateful to my former associates in Florida Power & Light Company's Law Department where I toiled for many years prior to my retirement: Attorney Jean Howard, who assured that my discussions on the troublesome technologies in the office place were as up-to-date as they could be, given the rapidity of change, and who also put the kibosh on a few anecdotal references where I got carried away and which might have caused negative reactions in some circles; Ted Blount, whose wise counsel and journalistic talent often kept my own excesses in check; and Ray Adams, a consummate claims manager, adjustor and investigator, who probably knows as much about corporate liability as any attorney.

Neither this nor any other of my literary efforts would ever have come to fruition without the patience, encouragement and love of my wife of forty-three years. On any given day, when five o'clock rolls around and my perseverence begins to flag, Bunny is always there with a hug, a kiss, and my evening's Scotch on the rocks. Sometimes I continue writing.

TABLE OF CONTENTS

Introduction

You liked the article. You'll love the book! More importantly, if you are in a decision making position anywhere in the business world, you need this book.

Several years ago, while still wandering the hallowed halls of Florida Power & Light Company's law department, I wrote an article entitled the same as this book. I recall vividly my struggle to limit anecdotal information and to keep the word count within the bounds of the publishers' requirements.

The article was first published in American Corporate Counsel Association's *ACCA Docket*. Thereafter, it appeared in Business Laws, Inc.'s *Corporate Counsel's Quarterly* and its *Law Department Management Adviser*, and, still later, in the *New Jersey Lawyer*.

What surprised and delighted me were the responses I received from readers. I was confident enough of the value of the message to reasonably expect a few compliments from friends and associates. As it turned out, call after call from major corporations and business organizations around the country—one from the University of Michigan wishing to use the article in its business administration classes—reached my desk, each requesting permission to copy the article for use inside the requestor's organization.

For anybody that has written anything for publication, I need not tell you how delighted

I was at the favorable reaction. Aside from the pleasant stroke to the ego, I was especially pleased my message had not fallen on deaf ears and that we could realistically hope for more prudent writing habits in the business community.

My purpose in writing the article in the first place was and still is, I believe, self-evident. My former associates and I, like so many other lawyers and claims adjustors in the corporate environment, had repeatedly over the years "pulled the fat out of the fire" for our employer and its employees, whenever they got involved in a claim or lawsuit whose inspiration, if not foundation, was a carelessly written note or letter or memorandum.

It seemed to be a never ending struggle, however, since there was always enough personnel turnover to assure that lessons once learned had to be retaught and reemphasized with new executives, department heads and their staffs. In the topsy-turvy, competitive, profit-starved business world today, managers are hired, fired and retired with seemingly blazing frequency. And the ever-increasing litigiousness in our society compounds the problems related to the recording of ill-chosen memos, comments and letters. All these changes make the prominence of this book on the credenza in every manager's office absolutely essential.

When I received the call from the University of Michigan, following my retirement, I realized the article's message was continuing to thrive even years after its initial publication. Obviously, the perils of imprudent writing were not going gently into the night.

This is when I made the decision to write this book, both to greatly expand on the details and anecdotal illustrations I could not include in the article and, also, to bring all the features of the article up to date. After all, e-mail and the Internet were merely subjects for casual conversation when the article was written, and other technologies were and continue to be in rapid transition.

So, here it is. I hope I am not being too immodest to say, if you found the article to be useful, then this book should be indispensable to you.

Good luck and happy, litigation-free writing!

—Ed Ahrens

Notes

Chapter One

Blame the Sumerians

The writer's art, of course, lies not in merely collecting words or in distinguishing among them. The art lies in stringing the right words together artfully.

—James J. Kilpatrick

The earliest and most universal means of communication available to human beings was speech and gesture. Back when chauvinism was still a way of life, when Ug raised his club over Um's head and muttered some unintelligible grunts, Um knew it was time to feed the old boy.

But at some point in the history of humankind folks developed a need to convey thoughts and feelings in a form that was not limited by time or space. Historians tell us the Sumerians in southern Mesopotamia were the first to perfect a word-syllabic system of full writing around 3100 B.C. The Sumerians, I suspect, were lawyers.

The Encyclopædia Britannica tells us that

Notes

"Sumerian is clearly an agglutinative language in that it preserves the root intact while it expresses the various morphemic changes, through the concatenation principle, by means of prefixed, infixed and suffixed elements." I wager those Sumerian dudes did not have as much problem communicating among themselves as we do!

Lawyers or not, and like it or not, we could not survive without utilizing the written word. We write to remember (or to not forget); we write to convey a message; we write to instruct—as I hope I am doing now.

But do we always write for the right reasons? I think not. And the semantic whipsaw of our legal system is ever ready to remind us of our blunders, especially when that unforgiving system focuses its attention, and its zeal for damages, on the written words of corporate executives, middle managers, supervisors and other employees. (While lawyers may not often be involved in purely domestic matters, emotional strife is also ready to strike family members, when they write letters or memos in anger or frustration.)

In our business and personal affairs, we write to communicate, to report, and to analyze. These are the right reasons. We could not imagine doing otherwise. In the chapters that follow, I will suggest to you that, too often, we write for the wrong reasons and, just as often, with the wrong motives. I will suggest some acid tests that we must pass in order to avoid

Notes

the sometimes unanticipated effects of what we write. And I also will identify the Writing Gremlins of the business world, each of whom relishes the opportunity to aid and abet those who have allowed their better judgment to lapse.

Notes

Chapter Two

I Could Write a Book!

"When he gets started, his tongue is like a race horse; it runs fastest the less weight it carries."

—Senator Carter Glass

We are all impulsive to some degree, especially when goaded by motives that we think are pure but, in fact, may be ill-conceived and wrongly implemented. Such motives include, but certainly are not limited to, the following:

To Impress the Boss —

"Look at me! I found twenty-five hazards around our company today!"

No discussion on the merits of the findings, no rational assessment of their seriousness, no suggested solutions, just pride in numbers and in data indelibly inscribed for posterity— and for the benefit of plaintiffs' attorneys. And that employee expects a raise or a promotion or at least an "Attaboy!" from his boss for his accomplishment.

Notes

Safety engineers or inspectors who are delegated the awesome responsibility to search out, identify and report safety and health infractions can be angels from heaven in preventing many serious accidents to employees and to members of the public. But there is a right way and a wrong way to carry out this important task.

No one person can always be certain he or she has accurately assessed a safety or health condition. Unless it poses a clear and immediate danger, some time and analysis is normally required to make a positive determination of a condition as being truly "hazardous." The difference is often one of perception as opposed to reality. And mass reporting of conditions not fully assessed or which cannot realistically be corrected immediately, is counter-productive. As often as not such action involves conscientious but misguided and short-sighted motives.

Recent "whistle blower" laws serve to protect the employee who in good conscience reports the commission or existence of a legal violation, safety related or otherwise, on the part of his or her employer. If the employee has discussed the matter with the employer and is acting within the framework of the applicable law, certainly I do not intend to include them in the group I am discussing here.

To Cover Your Tail (Better known as CYA) —

"Here's a list of fifteen defects in our construc-

Notes

tion program. Whew! Now, I've told you, so don't blame me if something goes wrong!"

You can spot this person. She is vigorously brushing the problem out of her soiled hands as she retreats down the hallway.

The CYA Memo-to-File is one of the oldest, and vilest, practices in the book. This employee is not going to get caught short by someone else's short memory. Rather than following up on action taken in response to her report of problems, she simply records them in a file. In the event of a warranty action on an equipment breakdown in her company, these hot little records await a legally enforced document production request, which will derail or at least greatly complicate such effort, to the utter surprise and dismay of her boss, her boss' boss, and on up the line.

Now you might ask, why should an employee catch hell for documenting the information after reporting it to her boss and being rejected? It's a tough decision, I admit, but, if she has the courage of her convictions, she will resign rather than surreptitiously plant a potential time bomb in the company's files.

Tell 'em, write 'em, and, if they do nothing, and you're sure of your findings, quit—assuming, of course, you don't fall under the circumstances contemplated by a whistleblower statute. CYA memos-to-file reflect a lack of guts and little potential for glory.

Notes

To Transfer a Monkey—

"Boy, this is really screwed up. You'd better fix it, or you'll be in trouble!"

And this person walks away confident that he has left that incriminating document, like a bloody dagger, plunged deep into the center of his reader's back. It is the sibling twin of the CYA memo-to-file, one level above the latter on a moral scale only because this potential time bomb is not secreted. The record, however, is still there and available to the world, requiring some action, if only to dismiss its validity (or the employee).

The wielder of this stiletto frequently prides himself in having assumed the authority to delegate responsibility for the problem. The consolation for this behavior is that such an employee rarely demonstrates lasting power. His alienated employees, if not his disgruntled boss, will show him to the door before he has wrecked their source of employment.

Some years ago, I personally received a copy, one of many, of a full-page memo regarding a "Fire Protection Inspection by [ ] Mutual Insurance." It was a report written with obvious pride by a local office employee. It stated, among other things, that:

- ❑"The amount of combustibles present in this particular office is *tremendous*"
- ❑"Due to the severe overcrowding of the facility, a *definite* 'life safety' problem for

the occupants now exists."

- "With the exception of [ ], no facility even approaches the *severe* overcrowding you have at the [ ] office."

(*All emphases are mine*)

A natural initial reaction to this memo might be one of admiration for a dedicated employee, and in fact his conscientiousness was probably never in doubt. It was his judgment that was in question. He did not know that this office already was scheduled to be relocated in the very near future and that the company did not own the building. The planned relocation proceeded in an orderly manner, and no one at any time was placed in danger. He was under informed, not only about the relocation but also about the risks he so vividly described. Note that he also throws in a dire reference to another facility, about which he says nothing more—and which also turned out to be baseless.

Nonetheless, if almost anything had happened in the building following receipt of his memo and which was the subject of his memo, if even casually related to the conditions he described, the company would have been placed in a difficult liability situation. What should he have done? He should have picked up a telephone and called the appropriate management personnel responsible for the building. No such effort was made by him.

Notes

To Force Something to be Done —

"Nobody would listen to my idea, so here it is in writing. The Company better fix it now, or else!"

First cousin to the CYA memo-to-file and frustration's last refuge.

I recall an instance when a middle manager at a major utility beseeched her top management to take action on an environmental matter. Her concerns were baseless in the opinions of other experts in the company, and, in fact, were clearly shown to be so by later research around the country.

When her proposal was rejected by an executive committee, which nonetheless expressed its appreciation for her conscientious effort, she was piqued and wrote an emotional, hyperbolized two-page memorandum to the vice president to whom she reported, with copies to several other department heads. The consequences of the existence of that memo became manifest in a personal injury action three years later. While the utility eventually prevailed in the litigation, the costly proceedings were greatly protracted by the seemingly incriminating questions raised.

A more dramatic and costly illustration involved a major investor-owned utility in the midwest several years ago. The state utility commission, during its review of a nuclear power plant project, unearthed internal notes quoting a senior company official's complaint, late in the project, that "we don't know where

Notes

we are; we don't know how we're going to get this job done; we must find a way." You can be certain that this officer had peers who regarded his comments as overstatements, and, obviously, he had a limited and designated audience in mind. Hyperbole or overstatement sometimes gets the job done more quickly, but it can be just as effective conveyed orally. Nonetheless, largely on the strength of those notations, the regulators disallowed $384 million of the plant's $2.98 billion cost.

It is hard to say which of these categories the writer's actual motivation fell into; there may have been multiple motives: CYA, transfer a monkey, or force something to be done. Whatever the writer's intentions, they clearly backfired.

To Vent Anger or Other Emotion —

*"Now I've gotcha, you *@#?*!"*

This person probably does not have the courage to engage in a rational conversation with, or even to face the target of his contempt, and, so, spins off his poisoned prose with no thought given to its possible incriminating effect, on himself, the other party (with whom he likely will continue to be working), or his company.

The "gotcha" is usually not as obvious as in the quoted illustration. Such a memo or letter often is infused with disarming sweetness. But the between-the-lines message is the same:

Notes

I'm better than you, and this proves it. Of course, it tends to prove just the opposite, and too often sows the seeds of dissension and discontent in an office, thus, through negative distraction, robbing it of the wholesome vitality needed for a profitable business.

Life, at home and in the business world, is full of one-on-one negotiating communications. This hothead would do himself a service by reading William Ury's book, *Getting Past No—Negotiating Your Way From Confrontation to Cooperation.*[1] Ury speaks of "hot buttons." Everyone has them; some have more than others; some have hair triggers. It's all a matter of self-control and employment self-preservation. As Ury says, there are times we need "to go to the balcony," i.e. to step back and reassess our reaction to an external stimulus.

To Show Off Your Literary Skills —
"Someday I'll write a book about all this!"

I've left the best for last. We all have known the creative scribe who says in five pages what could have been said in one...or less...or none. She has a thesaurus on her desk, a well-worn dictating machine on the credenza (or has mastered Word Perfect) and a secretarial candidate for carpal tunnel syndrome cringing behind a typewriter or word processor. Down deep in the scribe's heart, she feels she has missed her calling as Leo Tolstoy's successor.

This is the person who, orally, doesn't know

Notes

when to shut up, and, with pen in hand or fingers flying, doesn't know when to stop, or, as George Orwell once observed, is "like a cuttlefish squirting out ink."[2]

Every memo is a monograph, every letter a treatise. For her, the written word becomes a challenge and an opportunity to expound. The simplest problem blossoms into a world crisis. And, frequently, the verbal superfluity contains liability-prone land mines that will explode unexpectedly some day in the future.

Of course, it isn't only the frustrated author that resorts to this type of diuretic exercise. Many employees hide behind the written word because they believe they are unable to articulate orally and, to paraphrase the old wartime warning, are afraid a slip-of-the-lip will sink the ship.

Business writing consultant Dianna Booher observes, "A concise memo, letter, or report saves reading time, writing time, and secretarial time—not to mention paper." She cites the field supervisor, who, speaking of one of his subordinates, says: "When I glance down and see the signature, I want to throw the memo back in my 'in' basket until I have a full day to devote to it. No matter what the subject, he rambles on and on and on. I just don't have the time."[3] The supervisor might also have observed that he and his company just couldn't afford the risks inevitably birthed by one of those tomes.

Maybe we are also seeing the classic "busy"

Notes

employee who surrounds himself with mounds of paper hopefully as a means of job preservation. He is the one never seen scurrying down the hallway without a piece of paper clutched in his hot little hand. Just don't ever embarrass him by asking to see the paper—it might be blank.

Notes

Chapter Three

The Bottom Line

The most essential gift for a good writer is a built-in, shock-proof sh-- detector.

—Ernest Hemingway

Economics plays a major role in the business world of the written word. Leaving aside the perilous legal consequences of imprudent writing, the waste of time and the labor and material cost of transcribing and the loss of more constructive opportunities can, if not checked, diminish the profit margin of a company. If flagrant enough, it can bring it to its financial knees, even to bankruptcy.

In 1990, it was determined that the average memo takes 54 minutes to plan, write, and revise, is rewritten 4.2 times before it is sent, and costs more than $65. In today's dollars, you are probably approaching a C-note. Some executives find memos not only expensive but insidious and regard them as either a waste of

Notes

money or a tool for covering up errors. Paul Stevenson, CEO at ATI Medical, Inc., put it on the line to his employees: "We say, 'Choose between working here or writing memos,' and they get the message."[4]

When the average person looks at a memo or letter and is asked to evaluate its cost, the first reaction is to believe that there are simply a few lines on a single piece of paper, costing pennies perhaps. Even the drafter of a business letter seldom pauses to think about the chain of events she has set into motion, not to mention the opportunities she has created for legal peril. The scenario may go something like this:

1. Boss dictates contents on machine or to secretary.
2. Secretary walks into office, retrieves disk or belt from outgoing mail.
3. Secretary returns to desk, transcribes dictation.
4. Secretary takes typed letter into boss' office and slips it into incoming mail box.
5. Boss reads letter, prides herself momentarily on her literary ability, then proceeds to make changes.
6. Boss places edited letter into outgoing mail.
7. Secretary comes in, picks it up, returns to her desk for another round of transcribing (for the second, third, fourth, ad nauseam, time).
8. If final draft, she again returns it to Boss.

Notes

9. Boss signs it, places it once again into outgoing mail box.

10. Secretary retrieves letter, treks to copy machine, makes necessary cc's, returns to her desk, types envelopes, inserts letter and cc's therein, sticks stamps on all of them and places stack into her outgoing mailbox.

11. Office mail person picks up mail, places it into common receptacle, where it is picked up by building mail person, taken to mail room and, thereafter, delivered to post office.

Well, you get the drift. I won't even get into what goes on at the addressee's end. Some of this may have been made obsolete by the personal computer, but my experience suggests that things haven't changed that much. Only the job responsibilities are different. The potential for legal and financial exposures are not.

Dianna Booher offers the following eye-opening analysis of a typical "Joe Jabberwrite" earning "$35,000, or $17.50 per hour." As Booher says:

- ❑ Joe's writing the average report of 2 1/4 pages = $65.62
- ❑ Joe's report-writing task annually (50 weekly reports) = $3,281.00
- ❑ Joe's writing the average letter or memo (54 minutes) = $15.75
- ❑ Joe's letter/memo writing cost annually (1 per week) = $787.50
- ❑ Organization's annual writing cost for

Notes

1,000 employees ($17.50/hour) who write at least one 2 1/4 page report and one short memo or letter per week = $4,068,500.00
**Above calculations do not even consider clerical support time in typing, duplicating, or distributing—or reading time for those on the distribution list.*[5]

Also noted by Booher is the fact that 45 percent of all papers filed are duplicate copies and that the storage and maintenance of those duplicates and unnecessarily kept originals costs about $2,160 per four-drawer file per year.[6] I shudder to recall the number of such file cabinets in the department I worked in and to impose this annual cost to that number.

While wading through voice mail and being unable to speak to a warm and fuzzy human being might be aggravating, oral communication, in most instances, is still the least costly way to go—and the art and enjoyment of human contact is preserved for another day.

"Mend your speech a little," Shakespeare warns, "lest it mar your fortunes."[7] I say, mend your speech and your writings, lest they mar your fortunes—and, perhaps, place you in a costly witness chair.

Notes

Chapter Four

The Acid Tests

Nature, not content with denying him the ability to think, has endowed him with the ability to write.
—A. E. Housman

As a lawyer and mediator and a former corporate counsel, I know only too well that written words can have legal ramifications. In many cases, it is almost impossible to know in advance whether what you write in a business connection will come back to haunt you. But, if you want to have a pretty good idea whether to proceed with the document you have just undertaken to create, I suggest you put it to the following Acid Tests:

1. ***Would you send a copy to the chairman or CEO of your company? (Would it be suitable for his or her signature?)***

Close the door to your office and conduct a private role-reversal with the Big Boss. Put yourself in his or her office, behind the desk of

Notes

that ultimate decision maker. Separate yourself completely from your authorship of the document. You are seeing the copy of your letter or memo for the first time and, knowing that you have only a copy, realizing that the original at that moment is sailing to its addressee, if not already in those foreign hands.

Will you smile with satisfaction that one of your subordinates demonstrates superb literary skills, and excellent judgment as well? Or will you be in a panic groping in your bottom drawer for the Mylanta—or the .32 calibre revolver, uncertain who the target should be?

Now, if you were able somehow to cross that perilous threshold without suffering a peptic ulcer, take it one step further. If the letter is being proposed for your signature—remember, you are the chief executive officer with responsibilities for everything that goes on in your company and you are accountable to the board of directors and the stockholders—would you sign it without hesitation?

Give yourself time, even a moment or two, to reflect on how the letter will impress the reader. (So you don't miss the semantic connotation here, one car slamming into another leaves an "impression.")

2. ***Would you send a copy to the local newspaper, for all the world to see?***

If you have any reservation about sharing your words with the rest of the community, a

Notes

little red flag has just sailed up the pole. This is the stuff of lawsuits. Which is not to say that you dare not write anything you wouldn't wish to circulate to the local press. Obviously, there are many things we write, even if they might be of interest to that news hungry medium, that we would not copy them on, lest they become the seed for creative journalism.

Nonetheless, this test may prompt you to do a little rewording—just in case, or at least to weigh the consequences of having it leaked to them.

3. ***Would you send a copy to the agency or agencies that regulate the business of your company?***

Hardly any business today is completely immune from some regulatory oversight, whether it be a public service commission; the state insurance commissioner; the U.S. Securities and Exchange Commission; the state department of banking and financing; federal, state and local environmental regulators; and countless others.

You may regard these folks as meddlesome bureaucrats, but they have been charged by the legislatures to carry out their responsibilities in a diligent manner.

The only question then is whether your letter, should it come to their attention, will spark an inquiry, perhaps an investigation. Most businesses would just as soon not hear a word

Notes

from their regulatory watchdogs.

4. ***Would you send a copy to your chief competition, to the "other side"?***

Of course, you wouldn't give your competitor anything that was of benefit to them, would you? Or would you? Later, I will discuss one of the ways you might do so, unintentionally, but just as effectively. For now, however, consider the possibility that you get into litigation with your competitor or find your company defending itself in an antitrust action initiated by your competitor. Under either of these circumstances, your company may find itself disgorging documents it never dreamed of sharing with others, least of all its competitors.

Have you ever heard of a disgruntled employee? An unhappy ex-employee? Of course you have. If they leave your company, there is a distinct likelihood that they will remain in the trade or profession familiar to them and go to work for your competitor. And they can be and have been the couriers of almost any document the former employer might possess.

5. ***Would you be pleased to receive it from someone who works for you?***

Akin to 1 above, but here you are just you, and you receive such a letter or memorandum from someone working for you. It is forwarded

Notes

to you for your attention and action. Can you accept it as written? Or will you "red line" it here and there and call your subordinate in to discuss his literary shortcomings?

6. ***Finally, would you feel comfortable reading it, in full, while sitting in a witness chair in a steamy courtroom in a lawsuit against your employer—with your job on the line?***

Never happen, you say? Don't count on it. In the litigious society we live in today, the chances are very good you will have the spotlight someday, perhaps in a legal action by or against you personally, more likely in an action by or against your employer—which, incidentally, in the latter instance does not exclude the possibility of your being personally involved. While your employer may well be vicariously liable for acts performed within the scope of your employment, that does not mean you cannot be named as a defendant as well. While not necessarily a target for the recovery of damages, we are almost always personally liable for our own wrongdoings that cause injury or damage to another.

The situation here, however, is not whether you are liable but, rather, how you will be able to protect your employer (and your job?) against damaging evidence you have been instrumental in creating. The trick, long before that eventuality, is to read what you have written with that likelihood in mind. Now, how

Notes

proud are you of the words and phrases you have chosen? It is surprising how indifferent people can be to the negative significance of what they write. It may stem from the intensity of one's focus, a forest and trees dilemma perhaps, where the writer becomes so preoccupied with what he or she is trying to say that one forgets it is being indelibly recorded to last as long as the paper and ink hold up.

If you can honestly and comfortably answer "Yes" to all these questions, then you are probably okay. If you are still uncertain, I suggest you talk (don't write!) to your nearest friendly lawyer—or, perhaps a better alternative in certain circumstances, is to just let the dubious dispatch die a peaceful death in the round file or, depending on the extent of your unease, the shredder.

Notes

Chapter Five

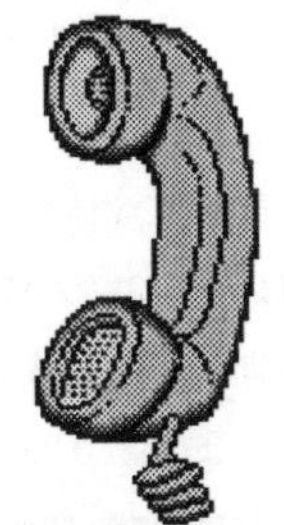

Virtues of the Spoken Word

A speech is like a love affair. Any fool can start it, but to end it requires considerable skill.

—Lord Mancroft

While not always appropriate, nor in some cases even advisable, there is a lot to be said for oral communications. An oral communication has two great features: it is of momentary duration and therefore restricted as to time (once the word is uttered, it's retained only by memory); and it can only be used by persons in close proximity to one another and is therefore restricted as to space or access.

Many years ago a Lutheran pastor delivered a sermon based on the assumption that the words of famous people of history, including the great prophets, even Jesus himself, might be recorded. The pastor alluded to a theory that, since every word ever spoken created sound waves and therefore still hangs in the air, someday, someone will devise a mechanism to capture and distinguish those words

Notes

and to identify their speaker. The effect on world societies would be dramatic to say the least.

Unfortunately—perhaps fortunately—the means for such recordation has not yet been discovered, and we still enjoy the luxury of faulty memories.

Oral statements, even as they occur today, are not trouble free. It is still good practice to watch what we say. Our words do in fact hang in the air for a time, and, depending on their importance, in listeners' memories even longer. On a more practical level, you may have to testify under oath in respect to what you have said, and you will not wish, nor will your boss expect you to be untruthful. There also are severe legal penalties for doing so. So, while you are using care in what you write, do not suffer the illusion that you are free to speak as you please without consideration of the possible consequences. The U. S. Constitution may guarantee us freedom of speech, but even the law does not allow you to yell "Fire!" in a crowded theater if there is no fire.

Notes

Chapter Six

The Writing Gremlins

If a thing goes without saying, let it.
—Uknown

So, we will and we must write. When we do take pen to paper, voice to dictator, or fingers to keyboard, the object is to weigh the possible consequences of what we are saying and, just as importantly, be prepared to defend what we say and to overcome the consequences that flow from what we say.

Document retention practices and procedures constitute a complex world in themselves, a challenging nightmare at best, and I will touch on them in a moment. However, where such procedures have not effectively disengaged us from useless and troublesome documents, we would be wise to remember the Writing Gremlins of the business world. As long as paper containing the written word exists, they are always there, lurking in the

Notes

dark corners of the desk drawers, the credenzas, the file cabinets, operating procedures, and the ever-burgeoning electronic wonders of the office world with their insatiable appetite for documented information.

These Gremlins await the unwary in drafts, reading files, electronic mail, word processors, fax machines, computers, personal files, problem analysis or quality improvement programs, and procedures manuals. In the next few chapters, we will review them in detail, in the hope that knowledge and awareness helps you to spot these little demons and thus beat them at their own game.

Notes

Chapter Seven

Stay Out of the Draft

"Where shall I begin, please your Majesty?" he asked. "Begin at the beginning," the King said, very gravely, "and go on till you come to the end: then stop."
—Alice in Wonderland

When we were young, our mothers warned us to stay out of the draft lest we catch a cold. We dread the circumstances under which fathers, sons and now even daughters might be subject to the draft into military service. In fact, the only good draft I know is that consisting of my favorite brew.

The draft we should fear in the business world is the draft of a letter or document that can become legal evidence as readily and as quickly as an original document and very often is more interesting than the final draft.

In the popular Broadway play, *Pippin*, there is a charming verse that begins: "Everything has its season, Everything has its time, Show me a reason, and I'll show you a rhyme."[8] Well,

Notes

every document change had a reason, each of them had its time, and you should be so lucky that its purpose was just to rhyme.

Consider the evolution of any business document, whether a letter, a report or a contract, from the moment of its inception to the ultimate finished product. The first cut is usually a rough one, nonetheless reflecting your initial, albeit tentative, thoughts and opinions on its purpose. A job begun is a job half done, remember? You sat and thought about the project for hours, maybe days, and finally resolved to put something, anything, down on paper. Okay, so far, so good. You now have a bunch of partially legible scribblings you are confident can be molded into a more intelligible second draft.

The drafting and redrafting of a document increases in direct proportion to its importance in your mind. I confess I have drafted some contracts and many letters no fewer than ten times. While in the process of doing so, I naturally retained the previous drafts, in order not to lose my train of thought.

The day finally arrives when you and, in the case of a negotiated contract, perhaps even the other party or parties, have agreed on a final draft of the document. Everything is signed, sealed and delivered, and you pride yourself on a job well done. Moments later, as you place an executed copy in your file, you note the two inches of drafts sitting in there, containing all those changes and deletions and additions, and the occasional, extemporaneous, cute comments in the margins, like: "They won't accept—try anyway" or "This'll make 'em sweat!" or "A throw-away."

Yessir, that was a lot of work, requiring all your talents as a writer, as a drafter of ironclad documents. Your boss will be proud of you—but—but how will he ever know how much effort went into it? Easy. He can always look at the drafts, right? Wrong! Imagine his pride in you, if these drafts come to light in a legally harmful way.

The day may come when, document drafts in your hot little hand, you will be asked to explain each modification, each cute marginal note, in agonizing detail. Your boss may have directed you to change a term or condition in a contract or letter, even though you strenuously disagreed with him. Such dissension within your company's management staff revealed in a marginal note could bring tears to your eyes in open court—and a sag in your company's stock.

As a practical matter, why save drafts of documents that have been developed into final drafts? Pride of authorship? Ridiculous. All you will have is a history of second thoughts, bumbling errors, thoughtless comments, and internal debates over terminology.

Throw them out!

Notes

Notes

Chapter Eight

Problem "Paralysis" Programs

Sometimes I think it sounds like I walked out of the room and left the typewriter running.

—*Gene Fowler*

QIP or quality improvement programs, problem analyses, brainstorming sessions, management by objectives—by whatever name they are called in your company, and for all their other legitimate virtues, constitute a mine-field for "wrong" writing. And rarely are the architects of these management cure-alls sensitive enough to the dangers to alert their corporate clients.

Almost all such management techniques involve a proliferation of documents—flip charts, minutes, "fact-finding" records, notes, memoranda, reports, et cetera, et cetera. The most vulnerable to prying, litigating eyes are those with titles like "Pros and Cons," "Adverse Consequences," "Policy Deployment Reviews," or "Root Causes." Often, teams are

Notes

created to carry out these programs, and, under the pressures of promised rewards and awards and of close management auditing, there is a zeal to record the "good" deeds.

Whether real or fancied, employees see raises, promotions, careers and job futures at stake. And therein lie the dangers of overwriting and excessive recording of activities, whether constructive, destructive, embarrassing to the employee or the company, or just plain dumb. "Dumb" comments or suggestions actually are encouraged by management so as not to inhibit anyone's spontaneous thoughts or ideas.

This is not to say that such programs are bad. In fact, they are not only good, today they are vital to the restoration of the internationally competitive quality in American goods and services. Moreover, when they involve the written identification, description and analysis of liability-prone problems, they can still be extremely worthwhile, provided: (a) there is an immediate implementation of a solution, and (b) there is a system-wide replication of the solution to a system-wide problem or defect. The lesson: Document solutions, not problems!

Notes

Chapter Nine

The Unread Reading Files

Anything that is written to please the author is worthless.

—*Blaise Pascal (1623-1662)*

I have long been curious about the characterization given these files. They are the extra copies of letters, memoranda and other documents typed by your secretary that are carefully preserved somewhere for future reference. They are intended as back-up copies, and occasionally they are useful in avoiding the reinvention of the wheel, when a similar circumstance calls for a similar document.

I have never known them to be the subject of a "reading" session, and, in truth, they are the secretary's CYA, not yours. I suspect, with rare exceptions, you will find a copy of whatever you have created in the working file, matter file, or case file, whatever you may call it.

What is intriguing about these files is that, being "personal" files, they frequently escape

Notes

the purview of a corporate retention schedule and therefore just as frequently enjoy eternal life. Their disposal usually coincides with a fortuitous "What the hell are we keeping these old things for?" to which your secretary will indignantly, and quite properly, respond, "Well, you never told me to throw them out!"

Check your company's retention schedules and see that such files are included—with a designated short life span. They are too often the forgotten mother lode of documents—and they can become invaluable assets for adverse parties in the legal discovery that normally accompanies litigation. It is not unheard of for an ancient letter to suddenly resurrect, for purposes of supporting a legal argument, a procedure or directive that has long since become obsolete or superseded. Will it destroy your company? Probably not, but the legal costs associated with arguing it away, not to mention your time as a witness to corroborate its valueless nature, might surprise you—and your boss.

Put these papers on a short leash.

Notes

Chapter Ten

E(gads!)-Mail

In a few minutes a computer can make a mistake so great that it would take many men months to equal it.

—*Merle L. Meacham*

The computer is a moron.

—*Peter Drucker*

And you thought that billet-doux to Mary in Records Storage was expunged when she signed off, didn't you? Chances are it wasn't. At least not entirely and not for a while.

When I first began to research the phenomena of e-mail in the office I worked in, the concept of a world-wide Internet was solely in the dreams of computer whizzes. What we have heard, read about and even witnessed in the last year or two regarding the outrageous abuses, some criminal, in such largely unregulated systems represents the macrocosm of e-mail. Unlike some problems that are imaginatively exaggerated to make a point, here we

Notes

have a seemingly monstrous problem that needs only to be shrunk to bring it home to the average workplace.

If you are on a main-frame computer in your company, your electronic communications could remain in that seemingly limitless memory bank for thirty days, or more. While such inter-office communications systems are state of the art, and becoming more sophisticated all the time, they are highly conducive to informality, carelessness and sometimes outright abuse. Obscene and shockingly candid comments are not unheard of.

Computer terminals play a psychological trick on us. Perhaps because they are physically located in the relative sanctity of our office, they create the illusion of privacy. They make us believe they are private, quick and ephemeral—all of which leads us into the habit of being informal to the point of breezy.

Our messages are too often too personal, involve too little forethought, and are transmitted too quickly. The fingers are in action before the brain is engaged. The result is a careless transmission with no thought given, at that moment at least, to opportunities available at the other end to save our message, to print it out, or to retransmit it to as many other addressees as the receiver's imagination or devilment allows, including, through the Internet, users outside the company. Also, printed copies are not always true duplicates of the originals. They can be doctored.

Notes

If your company uses e-mail—if it does not, its competitive days are probably numbered—more specific information on how to safeguard message privacy is available from the Electronic Messaging Association (EMA) in Arlington, Virginia, (703) 524-5550. EMA also sells a thirty-six page "Policy Tool Kit" for $45.

Another source of help and information is the Electronic Privacy Information Center, a non-profit research center that examines civil liberties and privacy issues in connection with new information technology. You can reach them in Washington, D.C., at (202) 544-9240 or through the World Wide Web at http://www/epic.org.

If you think these dangers are exaggerated, an article by Michael J. Patrick in *The National Law Journal*[9] offers some dramatic, eye-opening examples of where people and companies were hoist on the petard of their own e-mail:

> *During discovery in a discrimination lawsuit brought by a terminated employee, a supposedly deleted e-mail message from the company president to the head of personnel regarding the plaintiff was recovered, stating "Get rid of that tight-assed bitch." That comment cost the company $250,000 in a settlement.*

> *In connection with Atlantic Richfield Co.'s sale to Siemens of Arco's solar energy subsidiary, Arco employee e-mails were discovered stating, "We will attempt to finesse past Siemens the fact that we have had a great amount*

Notes

of trouble in successfully transitioning technology from the laboratory to the manufacturing floor," and "As it appears that [Arco's solar technology] is a pipe dream, let Siemens have the pipe." These e-mails contributed to Siemen's request for $146 million in a subsequent lawsuit.

The most famous example of such an e-mail message is undoubtedly that of Los Angeles Police Department Officer Lawrence Powell who, after the beating of Rodney King, sent an e-mail message on the LAPD system saying "Oops, I haven't beaten anyone so bad in a long time." Other e-mail comments by LAPD officers that came to light included: "If you encounter these Negroes, shoot first, ask questions later" and "Capture him, beat him and treat him like dirt."

Beginning to get the point? These were otherwise trained, sophisticated, if not too prudent, employees who, in a lapse of judgment, believed they had more privacy than actually existed. Lawsuits are constructed on the foundations of some of the hundreds of thousands of careless but carefully preserved e-mail transmissions.

One more thing. If you are of the impression that e-mail can be expunged upon learning of litigation, think again, unless you are looking forward to some severe personal, civil liability or might even enjoy examining the

Notes

interior of a jail cell for an undetermined period of time.

And, if the thought occurs to you that the plaintiff suing your company will have a frustrating field day searching your huge volume of retained e-mail messages, again, think again. Under the direction of your company's counsel, you and your company probably will have to conduct that search. Unless you have witnessed the systematic dismantling of productive and profitable projects rudely shoved aside by such expansive and time-constrained research—as a man once said, "You ain't seen nothin' yet."

Remember: E-mail communications are considered writing for legal discovery purposes; they can be transcribed on command by persons over which you have no control; and they often are retained for a time even after you have removed them from your terminal.

E-mail messages can now also be saved in files on the hard drives of all those they are sent to—and the addressees can, at anytime, pull them out and even change them.

E-mail may be the single most dangerous source of liabilities a company has—and, given the potentials of other cradles of liabilities discussed, that is saying a lot. It certainly need not be stressed that you should never send sensitive, confidential data by e-mail.

Jennifer Files of the Dallas Morning News sums it up nicely: "[O]nly on the Internet is it

Notes

so easy to send a private message to an unintended reader. Or thousands of them." She quotes Dave Menter, a cartoonist on comic electronic behavior—its popularity speaks for itself—as stating: "[I]f you don't want the world to read your mail, then you probably shouldn't send it."[10]

Who are you? Like Sylvestor Stallone's famous line, e-mail may respond, "I'm your worst nightmare."

(Wonder if that sweet note to Mary in Minneapolis was printed out and mailed to you know whom at home? Nah, she wouldn't do something like that...would she?)

Notes

Chapter Eleven

Beware the Spoken Word!

The man with power but without conscience, could, with an eloquent tongue...put this whole country into a flame.
—*Woodrow Wilson*

Joe Blab isn't going to be caught by memos, letters or e-mail, no sir. He knows the answer. He'll pick up the phone and call his party. The phone rings and he hears...

"Hello, I'm unavailable at the moment, but, if you'll leave a message at the beep, I'll be happy to call you back when I return to the office..Thank you...And have a good day."

Beep!

"Hi, sweetheart, just wanted to chat with you about that Warren contract. Think we can get together without old google-eyes looking over our shoulder? Boy, how'd we end up with a wimp boss like that? Call me, honey. No,

Notes

don't call me 'honey,' call me, honey. Ha, ha."

Sweetheart returns to her office. She takes her seat behind the desk, pushes the conference button on her telephone, and dials the number to receive her messages—just as Wimp Boss walks in. Sweetheart, justifiably, fumes over the familiarity. "Google-eyes" grimaces, nods, says nothing, and walks out. Need I say more? Guess who's now pounding the sidewalk.

While voice mail technically does not fall into the category of writing or a Writing Gremlin, it certainly has the same permanency, offers the same opportunity for dissemination and incrimination, and, in fact, can be readily transcribed. It is a Gremlin, written or not, and it involves a technology that begs for judicious use.

Notes

Chapter Twelve

PC's, Word Processors and Sloppy Floppies

The real danger is not that computers will begin to think like men, but that men will begin to think like computers.
—Sydney J. Harris

So you have trashed the reading files, and everything is once again under control, right? Wrong. Ask your secretary where she has stashed the floppy disks. You didn't think she was retyping those letters and reports from scratch each time you revised them, did you? Of course not.

Before I go any further, I will be the first to acknowledge the secretaries' role in the business office has changed dramatically in recent years, primarily in conjunction with corporate downsizing, reorganization and the use of personal computers. The *Wall Street Journal* states that, according to the Administrative Development Institute in Holland, Michigan, 71%

Notes

of secretaries now perform duties previously performed by management. According to the article, they typically work for more than one boss, too, "since companies now let only the highest executives have a private secretary."[11]

Nevertheless, even today, stenographers and secretaries frequently still use a word processor or a word processing typewriter, the older step-sister of the personal computer. And where the "boss" now uses a personal computer, he or she, too, is involved in the same preservation scenario. The use of this equipment allows them all to type only the first draft of the document, and, thereafter, simply slip the disk into the machine, retrieve the letter and edit in the changes you desire. And, along with the reading file we talked about earlier that has been growing over the years, the little, insignificant box of disks, containing megabytes of juicy data, is sitting in the credenza behind your or the secretary's desk awaiting the next request to produce in a legal action against your company. Another gold mine of documents.

When last did you or your secretarial staff consider how many and what kinds of documents were filed away on floppy disks? Do you follow a standard practice of backing up onto disks all the documents you create, thus retaining for someone's possible retrieval even those of no value as well as those you thought were expunged or destroyed? If so, it is time to rethink the practice.

Notes

Or perhaps your office is on a local area network (LAN) system. If so, your document may be stored, instead of on floppy disks, on your hard drive, your secretary's hard drive or on any hard drive in that LAN system. When last have you or your secretary purged your hard drive file? Do you know what safeguards, if any, have been established to prevent your work product from being stored on someone else's hard drive?

While we are on the subject of PCs, a *Wall Street Journal* article recently pointed out that "the meshing of company computers and the Internet has raised a bigger concern: unauthorized access from outside."[12] That threat of penetration, the article states, is currently well over 20%. All that said, the article devotes special attention to the thief within. In an era of corporate downsizing, growing employee insecurity and increasing workloads—not to mention whistle-blowing incentives created by federal law—"[p]ersonal computers [have become] the biggest contributors to the security headaches for companies...'[E]ase of use means ease of abuse,' says Richard Heffernan, a computer-security consultant based in Branford, Conn.'"

The WSJ article cites as an illustration of a company's vulnerability the case of a General Mills Inc. former food scientist who gained unauthorized access to the company's mainframe computer, after being passed over for a promotion. "He allegedly misappropriated

Notes

eight breakfast-cereal recipes, including those for Wheaties, Cocoa Puffs and Cheerios, and then quit to join a rival cereal maker." The information might just as readily have been on a personal computer, if only as a way station on its way outside the company.

Remember, a request to produce documents in litigation can reach data on disks and drives, and they may be more revealing than you ever imagined.

Notes

Chapter Thirteen

Just the Fax, Ma'am

If any man wishes to write a clear style, let him first be clear in his thoughts.

—Johann W. von Boether (1749-1832)

I have a very fine Hewlitt Packard fax machine in my home. It is used principally in connection with my work as an attorney and a certified court mediator, neither, in my semi-retired case, generating a great volume of transmittals. During the past few months alone I have received three errant faxes intended for someone else. One of them demanded payment of a long past due bill from a local company. Out of respect for what I imagined the sender would regard as a matter between it and the addressee, I have tried to forget the name of the deadbeat company. Alas, I will remember, and I will not be inclined to do business with them, should my need for that product ever arise. It also occurred to me that, if, as a courtesy, which I have done in the past, I were

Notes

to retransmit the document to the intended transmitee, the sender might find itself exposed to a claim of libel in light of my receipt and therefore publication of the dunning correspondence. I returned it to the sender.

The other misdirected faxes were not this significant, but you begin to get the idea how easy it is to unwittingly share your otherwise private fax message with the rest of the world. Think about it, one finger inadvertently hits the wrong key and the resultant number happens to be that of another fax machine. Voilà! A stranger is reading your document.

According to BIS Strategic Decisions, a market research and consulting firm, by the end of 1994 in the United States alone there were 11 million facsimile machines cranking out 47 billion transmissions, and that does not include 17.4 million personal computer faxes spitting out 8 billion more transmissions. Clearly, the fax is fast becoming a regular feature in both offices and homes. With the efficiency of the United States mail system seemingly diminishing in inverse proportion to its cost, it is no wonder that we are resorting more and more to the fax machine, a convenient and instantaneous means of communication representing a neat compromise between the plodding post and the much higher cost of long distance telephone calls.

Unfortunately, with the blessings comes the curse. The horrors of misdirected hard-copy messages have become legion. Consider the 73

Notes

million dollar judgment against a prominent national retailer for accidentally sending confidential information about a wholesaler to a competing wholesaler![13] Dial the wrong number and you may wish you had utilized Alex Bell's invention.

So, as with the other Gremlins, the objective should be to use this technological convenience with care and caution.

Notes

Chapter Fourteen

It's Personal!

No writer long remains incognito.
—E. B. White, The Elements of Style

For the attorney defending your company in a legal action, perhaps one of the most elusive and troublesome files is the "personal" file containing work-related or employee-related matters. This is the document or folder that you have slipped into your desk drawer or onto your personal computer at home or even on that top shelf in your garage. You know why it's there. Like Rosemary's Baby, you were concerned about it when it was created. But, of course, no one knows about it, so who'll be the wiser, right? Wrong again!

Unless you have a ragged moral fiber and, also, can feel snug in the belief that you will be able to deny the file's existence, somehow evade a legally warranted search of that desk,

Notes

or shelf, or home computer (and thus ignore the ugly perils of a judicial finding of contempt, or perjury, not to mention the other personal consequences often associated with such imprudent action), you would be wise to face the reality of its ultimate disclosure.

One of this Gremlin's offspring is a memorandum that is frequently requested of you by management. It is the sheet of notations related to a subordinate's behavior, supposedly both good and bad. It is intended to protect you, in the event future disciplinary action, including dismissal, has to be taken against the employee. It constitutes, you are told, a business record of the incident or incidents supporting your action. It is stuck away in a locked cabinet or drawer until such time it is needed, if ever.

The problem with this little document is that it usually reflects an event involving the confrontational passions of the parties, and its account too often resonates with the emotions of the writer. Overstatements, hyperbolic comments, perhaps even an occasional obscenity, could backfire and find you looking in the window at your former subordinate while you're standing in the unemployment line. In the worst case, you might find yourself on the receiving end of a libel suit. These memoranda are useful and helpful, no question, but great care and factual precision should be used in their drafting.

Consider it a rule: If you cannot live with the personal file, do not let it live at all.

Notes

Chapter Fifteen

Chapbook Dog

Procedures Manual: The Quintessential Gotcha!

Bill had left off writing...but he now hastily began again, using the ink, that was trickling down his face, as long as it lasted.

—Alice in Wonderland

A procedures manuals department can be a valuable corporate function in establishing and promoting efficient company operations. It also can be a hotbed of bureaucratic presumptuousness. If not monitored with the use of adequate reins, these otherwise conscientious folks can wreak havoc in a company by creating standards for everything from how to build a factory to specifying whether to have the toilet paper roll over or under. And, in so doing, they may lay the groundwork for self-imposed standards to which the company may later be held legally accountable.

Utilities, for example, are daily confronted with the task of keeping up with line clearance

Notes

needs, assuring that their lines, whether underground are overhead, are free from the interference of trees, which not only cause interruptions of service but, on occasions, involve a fruit picker, tree climber or trench digger coming into contact with a utility line.

The clearance task is horrendous and expensive, especially in subtropical areas, where arboreal growth rates—try tracking the root system of a ficus tree, not to mention its above ground growth—rival the fast forward on your VCR. Worse, the rates of growth vary greatly among the almost endless variety of trees, thus making it difficult to cut them in a uniform way and with uniform frequency, even assuming the utility can overcome homeowners' or local governments' vehement objections to any cutting at all.

I can recall many years ago a trade association presentation by a utility representative bewailing the defense costs associated with a personal injury lawsuit arising out of an alleged violation of its own manual of procedures.

There is hardly a utility that hasn't at one time or another had an overzealous manual writer attempt to set forth the growth rates and trimming frequencies of a company line clearance program. Not a bad idea in itself, except those folks often fail to consult with the operating department responsible for compliance and whose budget may not meet the rate of frequency specified, and, more importantly, who may have different views on the approach to the task. Result? Possible liability in the

Notes

event of an accident and truly a case of taking aim at one's own foot. All the work of the Procedures Manual Gremlin.

Not to be overlooked in this fertile ground for self-incrimination are a company's procedures for procedures development. Have no doubt about it, those departments do have internal procedures. They include who to contact for preliminary information, who to address as principle responsibility for the contemplated procedure or procedure change, who to include by means of copies and for feed-back, and, finally, to whom in upper management to circulate the penultimate draft for final approval.

It doesn't take much imagination to assess the number of copies and transmittals involved here, and the concomitant potentials for liabilities arising out of the saved-forever documents and the often rhapsodized objections or appeals for modifications emanating from the usually excessive number of addressees. Many of the latter are added upon receipt by the initial addressee.

The end work product of a procedures department can be the bane or boon of a company lawyer's career, depending on the lawyer's diligence in protecting the corporation against ill-advised procedures and in promoting constructive ones. Moreover, poor and overdone procedures manuals lead to poor morale, as employees gradually drift into an indifference to a proliferation of meaningless or petty procedures.

Notes

Chapter Sixteen

Copiers: Human and Otherwise

In composing, as a general rule, run your pen through every other word you have written; you have no idea what vigor it will give your style.

—Sydney Smith (1771-1845)

For constructive evidence, a copy of a docu ment can carry the same value as the original, if the latter is unavailable. For incriminating evidence, it can have an unexpected value to an opposing litigant, even if the original is available.

Machine copiers have become the curse of many offices, and, the larger and better heeled the company, the greater the curse. By the mere push of two buttons, Number (of copies) and Start, dozens, hundreds, of duplicate copies come spitting out the side of this monster. Are they needed? Very likely not in most cases.

You've heard the conversation many times: "How many copies do you need, Mr. Jones?"

Notes

"Oh, I don't know…er…well, give me ten or fifteen—just in case."

"Hm, sir, we only have eight copies indicated on the letter?"

"Ms. Smith, please. We may need the extra copies."

Ms. Smith thinks, hm, maybe I had better make an extra five—just in case.

It's just that easy. Earlier, I mentioned that 45 percent of all papers filed are duplicate copies. Not only are most of them not needed, but more often than not the extras are filed together in the same file, thus bulking the file cabinets, the cost of which has already been discussed. Manufacturers of copy machines and the paper they use are well aware of these loose office practices, but, even if so inclined, it is not their responsibility to correct them. It is yours.

What is interesting is that many offices, including the one I worked in, have developed methods for holding people and their respective departments accountable for excessive numbers of copies by requiring users to record on a pad at the machine the number of originals copied and the total copies of each. Interesting, because the purpose has to do with the cost and maintenance of the machines, not the much costlier exposure to liabilities growing out of the superfluity of copies and their careless dissemination and retention.

These machines also are freely used by recipients of letters, memoranda and documents, usually "just in case" of the holder's need for future reference—or for other less noble pur-

Notes

poses.

It is not within the scope of this book to go into the potential for copyright violations. They often occur in these unrestricted copying habits, and management is well-advised to place notices at the machines cautioning users about improper copying of published materials.

Rarely are letters written that need a wide distribution. In most cases, there is little need for most, or any, "cc's"—and even less need for the nefarious "bc," the blind copy that you want someone else to see but not your addressee. I would hate to count the number of letter copies I've seen later distributed to others bearing these dubious and suspicious initials. And, when they get into the hands of litigants, they can arouse all manner of suspicions—some well-founded. It is a practice that requires great care, especially in respect to the choice of a bc recipient.

It is not unlike caring for your home's landscaping. When you apply a fungicide or bug killer or fertilizer, you make certain it is applied in the amount and type appropriate to the particular plant or herbage and confined to that immediate area of the yard. If you do not, great damage can be done. Writing requires the same care. Never more than is necessary and only in those amounts and directed to persons having the essential need to know.

In a previous chapter, I discussed the many uses and misuses of e-mail and the fact that the recipient of e-mail can redistribute electronic correspondence to an endless number

Notes

of people. The sender, of course, can do the same thing, just as she can do with "cc's" in a letter. One is as bad and as risky as the other. Facsimile or fax machines are not immune from such abuse or misuse. They, too, have the facility for creating "distribution lists." These may even be worse than cc's, because they, like e-mail, can be set to automatically distribute selected documents to a predetermined list of recipients—in many cases, unaltered even when the entire list is unnecessary.

An equally useful, but equally diabolical feature is that of "polling" with a fax, allowing you to make documents available for others to retrieve by merely calling your fax machine. It is simply a matter of setting up the document you wish to make available to a certain group whenever they need it.

Obviously, all of these machines, not to mention their users, are capable of duplicating with an ease and convenience and speed that induce the massive proliferation of written material, often spirited away with no control over the number and identity of the eventual receivers.

It also is not a bad idea to stamp a "Do Not Duplicate" on a letter which, while not duplicated for the benefit of copy recipients, is routed, and to specify its return to the sender, preferably by a certain date. (But see p. 87) A pack rat has an obsessive impulse to machine copy every routed material he receives, so he "will always know what is going on."

Notes

Chapter Seventeen

"Oops! What Do I Do Now?"

An error is the more dangerous in proportion to the degree of truth which it contains.
—Henri Frédéric Amiel (1821-1881)

You've sent out a letter or memo that should never have been written, much less delivered. You've screwed up. You know it. What do you do about it?

This is a touchy subject. Some might say, you wrote it, live with it. But you can't do that. The harm that may be done to another's feelings, their feelings about you, the liability your company and possibly you might incur, if it falls into the wrong hands—any or all of these may prompt you to take whatever safe measures you can to retrieve the correspondence. Before we go any further into this, be aware that, in order to retrieve an ill-written document, you must have control over and knowledge of its movements and routings after it

Notes

departs your desk. To the extent you do not, you are at risk, a risk which nonetheless may be worth taking, depending on the feared consequences of the document's continued existence.

If it is written to someone you know well and trust and no other copies have been made, call her and ask that she return it for further revision and that, unless she has already done so, not to read it. If all this falls nicely into place, you are in the clear, once you are assured that the working file, the reading file and any processor disk or hard drive have been purged.

The less hoopla you make over its retrieval, the less likely memories of its contents will be stamped in the handlers' minds. The latter will always be a concern, given the necessity to tell the truth and avoid perjury, in the event a handler or observer of the document is asked about it in the course of some future litigation.

You may be asked if you wrote the document you were able to retrieve and destroy. Your answer naturally would be yes, with the explanation that it was rewritten as it now appears in the letter in evidence, or that it was disposed of because it was poorly drafted. In the latter case, upon being asked what it contained, you will relate its contents to the best of your recollection. Enough said.

When the document has been sent to a large number of people, you will have to think carefully of the consequences of not retrieving all the copies. One of your addressees may have

Notes

the habit of making a machine copy of the document upon the very call to return it. In the worst case scenario, you have an outstanding copy that gets into the wrong hands, and you and your company end up with the dual problem of a liability-prone document in evidence, along with the evidence of your awareness of its nature, as reflected in your failed attempt to retrieve it.

In other words, retrieval as a remedy for your screw-up, must be done right or not at all. In the latter instance, it may be better to write a "restorative" or clarifying letter or memo to all the addressees, duly apologizing for the "typographical error" or the erroneous and unintended statement or information.

And when and if the documents are retrieved, assuming you are so lucky, don't make the mistake of retaining them or your file copies, in order "to demonstrate that you made a mistake and got the letter back." Too foolish to mention? You'd be surprised. Lawyers are not smarter than non-lawyers; they just know more about the wily, sometimes illogical, ways of litigation and litigants.

Notes

Chapter Eighteen

To Save or Not to Save, That Is the Question

A sentence should contain no unnecessary words, a paragraph no unnecessary sentences, for the same reason that a drawing should have no unnecessary lines and a machine no unnecessary parts.

—*E. B. White, The Elements of Style*

It is ironic that with many of the Gremlins that are poised to get us into trouble, document retention guidelines seem always to come to mind as the first line of defense. And, indeed, when developed wisely, they can have exactly that beneficial effect.

On the other hand, if retention schedules are developed haphazardly, they can often cause more problems than they solve. There is a little pack rat in all of us. We are fearful of tossing that one document that we "know" we will be searching for in a couple of months. For some of us, exterminating the beastly little rodent requires the greatest self-discipline imaginable.

Notes

I know. I've been there. Any of my former secretaries—before my age of enlightenment, of course—will tell you, with shameless glee, how I stashed away papers and files. I believed that one resurrected document of value made keeping the stacks of garbage worthwhile—even if it was one out of thousands that never again came under the glare of a fluorescent light.

The danger in pack rattery is that it can, in some cases, be virtually incurable. Unless the retention schedules are assiduously audited, the incurable pack rat will ignore them—and your company may find itself involved in a document production order and in the embarrassing situation of denying possession of a document that in fact is holed up in the pack rat's office.

There are many documents—corporate bylaws, boards of directors' minutes, incorporation papers, to mention just a few—that must by law be kept for long periods of time, in some cases permanently. The truth is that most paper generated in the normal course of business by the many levels of the corporate organization need not and should not be retained very long. Setting those time periods can be a major chore, I admit, but it is worth the effort. It will save your company the considerable expense of storage, and quite possibly the expense of a liability or the legal expense of defending against one.

As an adjunct to auditing the retention

Notes

schedules, it also may be good management practice, from time to time, to offer employees assurance that, for the economic benefit of the company and even at the risk of losing a document that you may wish you had retained, it is better to err on the side of disposal rather than retention.

Notes

Chapter Nineteen

Trust, Mistrust and Anti-Trust

"Man does not live by words alone, despite the fact that sometimes he has to eat them."

—*Adlai Stevenson*

If litigation uncovers the foibles of imprudent writing, then the antitrust suit is the great disrober. No business executive that has borne the cruel, unforgiving ordeal of antitrust litigation ever again looks at courts, judges and attorneys in the same way.

And, forever thereafter, he or she will pay extraordinary respect, yea homage, to the lowly pen (or pencil, typewriter, word processor or computer).

The antitrust suit, with its treble damages and insatiable appetite for discovering documents long assumed to be sacrosanct, is often in the mind of the business man or woman, whenever decisions related to competition and competitors are pondered. It can turn the spine

Notes

of an otherwise proud CEO into jelly, line the pockets of attorneys with unimagined and unimaginable riches, and cause heads to roll.

The objective of antitrust legislation on both federal and state levels, ironically, is to protect trade and commerce from unlawful restraints and monopolies and unfair business practices—in effect, to protect small businesses from the sometimes voracious appetites and expansionism of big businesses. Are antitrust laws always enforced fairly and judiciously? Give me a break. This, after all, can be government bureaucracy at its finest—and operating in the judicial jungle at that. Unpredictable, unbelievably costly, and, occasionally, totally destructive of an organization.

While legal discovery in an antitrust case exemplifies the voracious appetite and can reach into the darkest, most distant corners of your business organization, it often focuses on merger documents, ad copies, training manuals, annual reports, submissions to analysts, requests for funds, planning documents, pricing documents, status reports ("Thing Pieces"), corporate minutes, and even trade association agendas and reports. Has anything been left out? Probably. Indeed, very likely.

Antitrust buzzwords find themselves on the blotters of opposing counsel, before presiding judges, and in jury rooms.

The legal eagles even have terms to describe the words that jump off the page for their review, leaving your attorney with a scowl on his face and opposing or government counsel beaming from ear to ear:

Notes

- ❑ Guilt Complex Words, such as "Destroy after Reading," "For Your Eyes only," or "No Copies."
- ❑ Power Words, such as "Dominate" and "Leverage."
- ❑ Planning and Intent Words, such as "Thorn in the Side" and "Intends to Dominate."
- ❑ And, finally, simply, Loose Words (generally about competition and prices), such as "Orderly Marketing," "Chiseler" (referring to the price-cutting competitor), and "Gentleman's Agreement."

Out of their contexts, many of these words—although probably not "dominate"—can have wholly innocent uses. In a context that hints at competitive strategy, they can be legally lethal.

Books have been written on the antitrust subject, and dealing with this swampland of legal exposure in any greater detail is beyond the scope of this book. Suffice it to say, the management of any major company, and probably many smaller ones, should be thoroughly familiar with the unique and costly perils lurking in the careless use of antitrust language.

Notes

Chapter Twenty

Don't Be Hoist with Your Own Petard

Read over your compositions and, when you meet a passage which you think is particularly fine, strike it out.

—Samuel Johnson

Good habits in the creation and retention of written documents are vital to your company's and your personal legal health. It is not my intention to suggest—nor would you abide by it if I did—that you cease writing or that you destroy all documents. That's absurd. We live by the written word; we simply do not want to die by it.

Imprudent writing and unconsidered retention are wasteful and costly. They breed confusion, clutter, and, yes, they can expose you and your company to legal risks that you might never have expected.

Robert Fulghum, in his marvelous bestseller, *All I Really Need to Know I Learned in*

Notes

Kindergarten,[14] reminds us that it is all very elementary:

"All I really need to know about how to live and what to do and how to be I learned in Kindergarten.... These are the things I learned:

....

- ❑ Put things back where you found them.
- ❑ Clean up your own mess.
- ❑ Don't take things that aren't yours.
- ❑ Say you're sorry when you hurt some body.
- ❑ Wash your hands before you eat.
- ❑ Flush...."

Without implying undue emphasis on the last of those items (indeed, you are obligated to freeze the impulse to dispose of any documents once you or your company become aware of the imminence of legal action relating to the subject matter of such documents), Mr. Fulghum in his unique and charming manner simplifies the considerations essential for proper social behavior. His advice is no less applicable to a good documentation process; it really is quite simple when you think about it.

I have no financial or other interest in the company, but I would be remiss not to recommend to you, as a vivid dramatization of the perils of imprudent writing, a 27-minute film produced by Commonwealth Films Inc.[15] Its title speaks volumes for itself: *Write Now/Pay Later*. My presentation of this film at the company I worked for brought home to the employees the importance of and risks associated with what they write and how those words might be interpreted months or even years later, including by outside sources and in court.

Recently, *The Miami Herald* featured an article on the disastrous 1961 Bay of Pigs invasion. In it, Herald Staff Writer Christopher Marquis cites a Central Intelligence Agency memo which refers to orders that "discussion of the assassination of Cuban leaders should not be put in writing."[16] Beam me up, Scotty! If the Mount Olympus of espionage and covert operations does not recognize that writing a memo not to write a memo is still writing, we are indeed in deep trouble.

You love to write? Fine. Commendable. Just beware that you don't be hoist with the petard of your own false elegance.

Notes

Notes

Chapter Twenty-One

Write for the Right Reasons

His style has the desperate jauntiness of an orchestra fiddling away for dear life on a sinking ship.

—*Edmund Wilson*

Dianna Booher's objective in writing her books—as well as in holding her seminars, one of which I was pleased to attend—is to show readers "how to write your way to success in business,"[17] and she is doing a fine job in promoting that objective. I commend to you her books and her seminars.

My goal is related, perhaps adjunctive, and yet it is different. If I am able to steer readers away from the legal quicksand that a misguided or improperly written document can suck them into, then my objective is realized—and, coincidentally, so might that of Ms. Booher.

As you get set to place pen to paper, or voice to dictation, or hands to the machine—computer, word processor, fax—think about what

Notes

you are going to write, why you are writing it, and how you propose to write it. Think about how it may be interpreted or used by others, either intended addressees or unintended receivers. Make sure it is for the right reasons, and put your product to the Acid Tests. Anything that survives this process is bound to produce the desired results and to minimize the undesirable side-effects.

As a lead editorial in *The Miami Herald* points out: "The electronic age, which has poked its unseen eyes and ears into every corner of private life, has led to the recording of some of life's tiniest, most casual moments.... Big Brother may not be watching you. But he may be downloading."[18]

The pen indeed is mightier than the sword, and the wounds inflicted, and self-inflicted, can be as damaging.

Notes

1. William Ury, *Getting Past No—Negotiating Your Way from Confrontation to Cooperation* (New York: Bantam Books, 1993) 43
2 . Ed Grimm, "Watching Our Language," *Think*, IBM Corp. 1987
3. Dianna Booher, *Would You Put That in Writing* (New York: Facts On File, Inc., 1983) 3,4
4. "Don't Write That Memo!," Executive Calendar (Workman Publishing Co., 1/90)
5. Dianna Booher, *Cutting Paperwork in the Corporate Culture* (New York: Facts on File, Inc., 1986) 24
6. Booher, *Cutting* 153
7. Grimm, "Watching"
8. Stuart Ostrow, *Pippin*, Motown Record Corporation, M760L, Hollywood 1972
9. Michael J. Patrick, "E-Maid Data Is a Ticking Time Bomb." Reprinted with the permission of *The National Law Journal*. Copyright, 1993, The New York Law Publishing Company: 14
10. Jennifer Files, "Be careful with your e-mail" the *Miami Herald* 18 December 1995: Business Monday 29
11. "Work Week," *The Wall Street Journal* 26 September 1995: A1
12."Why Many Businesses Can't Keep Their Secrets," "Marketplace," *The Wall Street Journal* 20 Novem ber 1995: B1
13. Geoffrey Tomb, "The Personal Fax," *The Miami Herald*, 16 February 1990: B1
14.Robert Fulghum, *All I Really Need to Know I Learned in Kindergarten* (New York: Ballantine Books, 1989) 4
15.*Write Now Pay Later*, videotape, Commonwealth Films Inc., Boston 1983
16. Christopher Marquis, "Behind scenes after Bay of Pigs: JFK snubbed Che," *The Miami Herald* 29 April 1996: A1,A8
17. Booher, *Would*
18."Before you hit the 'send' key…," *The Miami Herald* 16 January 1993: 26A

About the Author

Edward P. Ahrens, Jr.

Ed Ahrens was born in Hamburg, Germany, in 1934 and came to the United States in 1939. He presently lives in Miami, Florida, and has been married to Kathleen "Bunny" Van Buren Ahrens for 43 years. They have two sons, Edward III and John Michael, who, with their loving wives and children, reside in Tampa, Florida.

Ed received his Bachelor of Arts and Doctor of Laws degrees from the University of Miami in Coral Gables, Florida, and, also, is a graduate of Columbia University's Senior Executive Program in Business Administration.

Ed is an attorney in Miami, Florida. In 1993, after forty-two years of service, he retired from Florida Power & Light Company where he was its managing and senior attorney and assistant corporate secretary. He was a charter member, president and director of the South Florida Chapter of the American Corporate Counsel Association; president of Southeastern Claims Association; and chairman of the Claims Committee of Edison Electric Institute.

He now divides his time between mediating legal disputes and freelance writing. He is certified by the United States District Court for the Southern District of Florida and the Florida Supreme Court as a court mediator, is on the American Arbitration Association Panel of Arbitrators, and is affiliated with Florida Mediation Group, Inc. He writes short stories, essays and articles and is a member and vice president of the South Florida Chapter of the National Writers Association. He has been published in the Chapter's *Author's Voice Newsletter*, to which he contributes regularly, and in the American Bar Association's *Barrister*, the *ACCA Docket*, *Mediation Monthly*, *Innisfree*, *AIM* and *Sun and Shade* magazines, as well as in various publications of Business Laws, Inc. and The Florida Bar.

Order Form

Fill out this form to place your order. Mail orders should be addressed to Van Buren Books, 12001 S.W. 73rd. Avenue, Miami, Florida, 33156.

Title	Price	Quantity	Cost
The Perils of Imprudent Writing	$15.95		
		Subtotal	
		6.5% Tax (Florida only) *	
		Shipping	
		Total	

Shipping:
$3.50 first book.
$1.00 each
additional book.

* Residents of NY, NJ, PA, CA add applicable sales taxe

Please send me my copy (or copies) of *The Perils of Imprudent Writing* as indicated above. I enclose my check or money order (not cash), plus postage and handling

Business Name (When applicable) ______________________

Your Name ______________________

Street ______________________ Telephone (   ) __________

City ______________________ State_____Zip__________

For faster service, call (305) 232-0913

Fax (305) 232-9823

E-mail EdAhr@aol.com